Gareth's Pets

I realise I probably post too much about my pets who own me (I certainly don't own them!), but I hope reading the following may give you a smile.

Every night before going to bed I have a glass of milk. Some milk is put into the animals' food bowl. Whichever animal comes into the kitchen first gets it.

This evening the cat was first. She was happily drinking away until the dog realised what was going on, and came into the kitchen. He shoved her out of the way and started drinking the milk himself. The cat stood next to him. If you've never seen a cat with a miffed expression, you should have seen her this evening! Then he decided - before finishing it - that the call of the garden before bed was too much, and that he needed to go out to do what a dog has to do. As soon as he went out for a pee, the cat finished the milk before running outside to go a-rodenting. Should you never have seen a cat looking smug, you should have seen my little Madam this evening when she licked up every last drop, knowing that she'd won over the dog!

Should you never have seen a dog looking utterly forsaken, you should have seen the look on his face when he realised the cat had finished all of the milk whilst he was outside.

Should you never have seen a human grinning from ear to ear with the antics of the pets who own him, you should have seen me!

Incidentally, without the cat knowing, the dog has had another bowl of milk.

***

This morning at around 2 a.m. the dog barked at me (I'd fallen asleep on the sofa) as he'd decided that he desperately needed to be let out of the back door. Once I'd got there and opened it for him, he had a pee immediately outside on the steps (gee, thanks, mate!). Then he decided that a patrol around my back garden was in order, so walked down the first set of steps with me quietly watching from the back door.

I then noticed from the bottom of the garden (which is on several levels) the sensor-operated lights I'd installed for him to see his way up and down started lighting up one by one from the bottom upwards. Evidently a creature was coming up the steps towards him. I guessed that it was Scaredycat, who for some reason tries to pretend she doesn't like him when she knows daddy is watching. She evidently didn't realise that daddy was quietly watching at the back door.

Scaredy and Milo sniffed each other, and then spent around five minutes rubbing and licking each other, before trotting down to the bottom of the garden together.

When they both started coming back up the steps, I retreated inside. Scaredy for some reason tries to "save face" by feigning dislike of the dog! She wouldn't have come in with him had I been around.

Once they were inside, she pretended that she wanted nothing to do with him.

I get a huge amount of pleasure from my pets and their unique characters.

***

My dog has developed a new way of telling me when he wants some food. He picks up his food bowl and carries it from the kitchen into the lounge to me. I tried taking a photo of him earlier but, by the time, I'd got my mobile 'phone ready, the daft fella had bitten into the plastic bowl very enthusiastically in order to prove a point, and had broken it!

***

My dog is evidently a better teacher than I. Yesterday I erected a fly screen (one of those with a magnetic strip in the middle) on the utility room door which leads to the back door. I have been working hard on showing my daft little cat how to get through it, but without success. All of a sudden, the dog creeps up behind her whilst she's looking at it with a puzzled expression whilst I'm trying to show her what to do, and lets out a loud bark. She shoots straight through it! One minute later, and she's come back in through it. She's worked it out. Well done that dog!

***

My little Scaredycat in her new favourite place. She knows she shouldn't jump on the furniture, but pleases herself nowadays. (Any friends visiting for food, please note that the dishes below her will be put through the dishwasher before use! The dog suggests putting the cat through the dishwasher anyhow!

***

I've just been telling my friend Petra about a holiday I had when I was a young lad. My parents and I sat at a table next to two others on another table. The woman was very Northern, and repeatedly said "Aye" and "Oh aye" loudly as the man spoke. I couldn't resist imitating her, so repeatedly did the same - despite my unfortunate and embarrassed parents desperately trying to shut me up!

But the funnier thing is the effect that saying "Oh aye" has had on my little Scaredycat! She ran and jumped on my chest as soon as I said it, and purred loudly. Each time I said it afterwards she lifted her back leg and looked at me adoringly. It's obviously somehow a sound she loves.

***

I realise I probably post too much about my pets who own me (I certainly don't own them!), but I hope reading the following may give you a smile.

***

I wonder if telepathy is a thing. Earlier this evening I was about to get into my friend Petra's car to visit the home of a couple of family members which I'm looking after whilst they're away. I heard my adored - but sometimes utterly diabolical! - Scaredycat howling. I insisted on going us back inside and out into the back garden to check that she was ok. She was right at the very bottom of the garden (where I really couldn't have heard her, as it's a long distance from the front of my house) objecting to a bird in one of my trees who was too high up for her to climb and attack (although Petra said she'd got about ten feet up!).

Having been a cat who mostly stays in the back garden, she's now taken to appearing when the car returns in order to be let in through the front door.

She has now been fed twice since I returned this evening, and is on the lounge table in front of me demanding more. And she knows she's going to get it!

***

Today at the church where I'm privileged to worship, during the announcements at the end of the service, a birthday was announced, and we were asked to sing 'Happy birthday to you'. I was told that it was for somebody else in the congregation when I said I hoped it wasn't for me. But - lo and behold - it turned out to be for my forthcoming birthday, as I was unwell for my 50th last year and unable to attend. So they celebrated it almost a year late!
A huge amount of subterfuge had taken place to hide the cake by another assistant organist and smuggle it into church, for one of the assistant organists to play (who had asked if he could play the final hymn and voluntary - as he had known what was happening and wanted to play for it, and totally fibbed about wanting to play for the final hymn and voluntary! 😊), for a card to be signed by various folk (which was apparently hidden whenever I was around!), &c.
So I ended up duetting to 'Happy birthday to me' with one of our brilliant assistant organists, and going full 'theatre style' for some fun! Lots of kind people came up afterwards for handshakes and hugs.
The cake was delicious too! That was the icing on the cake! *groan!* I was saved a small piece, as they all apparently dived in like gannets!
I am very fortunate indeed to be part of a lovely community of friends.

***

RIP to Celeste, the last of my hens to have been named after organ stops. She was granny of the flock, and reached the very old age of eleven. Yesterday she was running around quite happily and enjoying treats. A sweet creature as far as little dinosaurs go; when a new hen was being bullied by the others a few years ago, I got her out of the pen to be with Celeste, who put herself between the bullied hen and the others, and looked after her, making sure none of the attackers could get at her whilst they both ate together (Celeste was boss hen, being bigger than the others!).

***

My adorable dog Milo goes upstairs with his daddy to bed each night. He and the cat used to take it in turns - i.e. if the cat arrived before him and he tried to get up, she'd thump him until he retreated downstairs! Nowadays she sometimes joins us, and snuggles in.

Milo and his dad snuggle together under the duvet, and daddy gently cuddles and fusses him until he goes to sleep. Then daddy prepares for sleep himself. Quite often Milo suffers bad dreams and starts whimpering, making other funny noises and twitching. Daddy gently wakes him (it can take a little while), and he pushes himself into me even harder - as if to say, I think, "Thank you, daddy for looking after me".

***

I often fall asleep on the sofa during the daytime. I'm told that I also make 'funny noises' and snore, and that Milo looks concerned, and comes to me to wake me up. Unfortunately, his preferred and somewhat inept method of doing that is to lick my face! He does that to me during the night too, causing me to rush to the bathroom to clean up my face. My lovely dog and I look after each other, and are the very closest of pals.

***

Here's a photo of my little Scaredycat when she was a kitten. She came in from out of the cold to my friend Petra's home as a little feral from a long line of village ferals. She is pictured with her late 'mummy', the much-missed Jacob who adopted her, and .taught her to be the best dog he could! I went up to Anglesey for a week to try to tame her, as she wouldn't go near humans. When Petra subsequently visited Devon for a few weeks, she brought Scaredy with her. Scaredy was so stressed by the journey that this became her forever home rather than her having to endure it again. It took Scaredy several weeks of looking out of my bedroom window before she was brave enough to venture into my back garden.,I've 95% got her tame - but you wouldn't believe so by the noise she made earlier when having a new flea collar fitted.

Jacob and his best friend!

I Am Owned by My Pets

It's now 3.30 a.m. and I awoke on the sofa around thirty minutes ago (which happens a lot nowadays). I felt peckish, and decided to have a little soup before retreating upstairs to bed. Scaredycat obviously heard me from the garden, and bashed her way through both cat flaps from the garden into the kitchen, squeaking to be fed (she is the most demanding cat I've ever known!). She jumped up onto the little unit I have in the centre of the kitchen where I keep my chopping boards and squeaked at me. I put her back on the floor. She jumped up again despite being told not to. I put her back on the floor again. So she jumped onto the worktop (fortunately the one where the dishes which need washing up are kept - I shall disinfect the chopping board in the morning) and insisted on being fed, despite devouring several sachets and bowls of biscuits each day! I carried her to her food bowl in the lounge (she likes daddy to take her to her food rather than doing the little jump from the armchair to the hi-fi unit herself) and fed her. She's become rather 'eccentric' recently, with liking to sleep on my napkin on the dining room table, or on one of my speakers. So the plump little madam had yet more food. I returned to the kitchen.

The plump little dog decided he wasn't going to be left out, and demanded yet more food, which he received. Then he demanded to go outside. So I unlocked the back door, and told him to go down to the garden for a pee. He decided he wanted to pee outside the back door instead. The area was cleaned only yesterday as he'd made it smell. He wagged his tail, came back in, and demanded yet more food. So he had some Melba toast.

The dog and I are going upstairs to bed. He snuggles up to his dad, and we fall asleep with me fussing him. Should there be such a thing as reincarnation, then I'm coming back as one of my plump, spoilt, demanding - but totally adored (as they know only too well) - little pets!

***

My hugely adored little dog - Milo - gets some exercise twice a day on the stairs before getting fed. My mobility isn't so good nowadays and I'm unable to take him far along the road, so I send him up and down the stairs. He has 'his place' which is on the landing halfway up. As well as understanding 'Go to your place', he also understands 'Top' and 'Quick'. He knows what he's being asked to do.

Getting him going is difficult, though. He looks at daddy, and his face says 'No'. His tail gives the game away. He loves playing up for his dad, and thinks it great fun!

When I offer him food and say 'Go to your place' he walks to the front door to ask for a walk in order to defray matters, or will go to the lounge to have a drink of water (which I call fortifying himself). He will then have a good stretch, (which I call limbering up).

Eventually the lovely little plump thug will realise that he's going to have to run (I don't think he understands when his daddy fusses him and tells him that daddy's only doing it to keep him fit). And then he goes absolutely mad running up and down the stairs, wagging his tail all of the time, and enjoying it all. He barks at me at times when I say "Up", but keeps running!

This only happens at his main meal and his treat in the evening. His other meal he doesn't have to run for.

On the odd occasion where I haven't told him to run for his main meal, he's looked quizzically at me, and has repeatedly run up and down the stairs on his own before eating!

***

It is now very late (3 a.m.). I spent much of the afternoon and then the evening asleep on the sofa, tired from yesterday's activities. I woke up sufficiently to see the cat jump onto the armchair where the dog is sleeping and to settle by him. She wasn't aware that I saw this. She's a funny little Madam; she can cope with one other person/animal around her - but struggles with more than one, unless the other is asleep! She snuggles up to the dog on my bed at times, but moves away from him when she realises I'm awake.

***

I woke up a little earlier on the sofa and replied to an email and sent a message to a new Facebook friend. The cat slept through it. She then woke up and demanded food - once she'd realised the dog was snoring and fast asleep. She's now returned to be next to him, realising he's in the land of nod. When he wakes up (if that's before I go to bed in a few minutes' time), I can see her running out through the cat flap I had installed in the lounge door for her as she'll have 'person overload' should she realise the dog and I are both awake! She's an eccentric little creature - but so is her custodian! She won't be happy when daddy wakes the dog in order to take him up to bed, and will probably run off outside in order to search for rodents (poor rodents - though she's thankfully less good at catching them now that she's getting older!)!

***

The joys of being owned by a cat

It's now turned 2 a.m. After church yesterday morning, I went home, did a couple of chores, sent an email, and fell asleep on the sofa. Sleep was interrupted occasionally by not only the cat, but also the dog jumping on me (he's a weight, but I suspect that's because I feed him too much). I briefly caught up on more email during one of the interruptions, and then fell asleep again. Madam (the cat) is the most demanding little beast you could ever come across, and frequently demands food and/or attention throughout the day! She has a tendency to thump me when she wants feeding or fussing (I find little scratches on my legs and hands which I realise were inflicted by her!), and then to squeak at me. I feed her on the hi-fi unit so that the dog cannot pinch her food (possibly more for his benefit than hers, as she'd probably thump him if he tried!). Most times I have to carry her to the unit from the armchair next to it, which is just a tiny jump which she's perfectly capable of doing should she want to.

So, at 2 a.m. I get woken by squeaking! Madam has climbed onto the dining room table (where she's not really allowed, but she rules the roost here; I don't get much say in the matter) and has settled on my napkin. She then knocks my napkin onto the floor when she realises she's managed to wake daddy, and I realise that with a cat having slept on it and now being on the floor, it will need washing. The washing machine went through a load after church. But now Madam wants even more food and is loudly demanding it! So daddy carries her to her food bowl, fills it with food, and she tucks in. Daddy remembers that he hasn't wound up the dining room clock (which he does every Sunday evening if he's not fallen asleep on the sofa), and then rectifies matters. He dumps his napkin back on the table, remembering that he must take his napkin holder off before it gets washed.

Daddy winds the clock, turns around, and finds his little princess has eaten her food, and has curled up on his napkin again, squeaking at him in order to demand a tummy tickle. He knows when he's beaten!

***

My plump little dog Milo gets diet pet food ordered for him from tails.com, as it seems to provide all of the nutrients he needs. They emailed the other day to ask if he'd lost any weight yet (he's been on their diet food for quite a long time) and seemed bemused that he still hadn't. I suspect I may know the reason why...

This morning I was having a bit of a sort out of the freezer. I reached out two pork trotters, defrosted them, and cooked them for him; they were simmered just sufficiently to kill any trichinella but not enough to soften the meat nor to soften the bone. He had one of them with his supper, and he looked like a dog who had had all of his birthdays come at once whilst he spent the next twenty minutes halfway up the stairs eating it (to where he goes when I say "Milo, go to your place!", and to where he goes when he tells me he wants food!).

***

Due to having a sore throat thanks to a nasty cold bug, I decided for supper to have a cold quiche, and some cold carrots and mange tout I'd cooked yesterday to help cool and soothe it. The carrots had come from a large bag of batons which had been reduced to pennies at the supermarket. I have never eaten cold, cooked carrots before, and expected them to be quite foul. They were!

 So I put one of those which I'd left in Milo's bowl in the kitchen and called him. He sniffed and looked at it with very mixed feelings, but eventually reluctantly accepted daddy's encouragement to eat it. He did the same with the second. With the third, he decided that they were actually quite nice, and I gave him the rest which he wolfed down. My dog is a living dustbin with a very waggy tail! He has rewarded me for this by sitting next to me on the sofa, cuddling up to me, and breaking wind on a frequent basis.

***

This has been an interesting evening - thanks to my beloved little Scaredycat!

Scaredy was a little feral from a long line of village ferals in Anglesey who adopted my friend Petra's home (who Scaredy wouldn't allow near her at first), and who I went up to Anglesey for a few days to tame (i.e. bribed the little cat with food!). After taming her - or so I thought - she went to the vet to have vaccinations. It was the vet's first day after training. Scaredy totally duffed her up and the vaccinations had to be abandoned, and I had to put her back in the cat carrier and take her back to Petra's.

To cut a long story short, Scaredy moved to Devon. But she hasn't quite forgotten her feral ways!

Earlier this evening Madam was in the hallway by me and she let out a howl. I was concerned, and wondered what was wrong. Later on she did the same, and I found that she'd put a leg through her flea collar.

Attempts to gently get her leg out of the flea collar were met with full scale warfare including claws and teeth, before Madam fled outside, still wearing her collar.

After lots of calling for her, Madam eventually crept in, and I heard her creep up to my bedroom. So I went up armed with a pair of scissors, and closed the door behind me to prevent her escape.

Have you ever tried to get a collar off a formerly feral cat from a long line of ferals, dear reader? After spitting, howling, claws and teeth, her collar was removed at just before midnight. You'd think she'd be grateful for the help, but not Scaredy! On the plus side, she's reminded me that I need to check the status of my tetanus jabs. And to buy some more plasters.
Tomorrow I need to put a new flea collar on my much-loved little girl. Gulp!
Would anybody like to buy a cat? One careful owner, very gentle disposition, and (possibly!) comes with a new flea collar. Price negotiable - but I'm willing to pay quite a lot.

***

My Parents and Other Animals

My mother and stepfather treated themselves to two new smart telephones before their recent holiday (which celebrated two significant birthdays) in order to take videos.

Tasked with the job of putting the videos onto a memory stick in order that they can keep them and view them on the television, I popped up to see the aged pair this afternoon. Imagine the hilarity which ensued when we discovered that for half of the videos, my mother had for some reason switched on the 'phone's camera before turning the 'phone upside down to record. And, no, they didn't visit Australia! Here's a photo of them trying to work out how best to turn their TV upside down.

***

I have just been watching an old episode of 'Mock The Week' on the television. Milton Jones said he had recently changed the lock on his front door in order to try to frustrate any burglars who might arrive by barge. I thought it very amusing, and I shared it with my friend Petra. She didn't get it at all, even with me repeatedly explaining about locks, canals and barges. That was even more funny than the original joke, and she still hasn't got it!

***

I was musing earlier on the value of friendship, and thinking how fortunate I am to know some really lovely people. Yesterday afternoon I went to my lovely friend Margaret's home again, with equally lovely friends Petra, Ivonne and Malcolm, and enjoyed afternoon tea and their company greatly. Along with great conversation, we each read a chapter of Petra's most recent book, and enjoyed much merriment. Another terrific friend - Mike - said he was so disappointed that he'd had a prior engagement and wasn't able to attend the invitation. But we've enjoyed each other's company over a couple of meals in the last week.

Treasure your friends, dear reader, and let them know how much they're appreciated.

***

This afternoon I popped up to my mother and stepfather's home to give my stepfather his present and card for his birthday tomorrow. I was kindly given a cup of tea. I noticed a fruit fly trying to swim around inside it, so went to the kitchen to get a spoon to reach it out.

My stepfather decided he would do it instead of me, and somehow managed to divide the fruit fly into two halves. I don't think the fruit fly was very impressed. He then inadvertently managed to get the two halves of the former fruit fly to sink down into the tea.

So I was left with a mug of tea with two halves of fruit fly in it. I've told them that my diary is busy for the next twenty years or so should I have an invite from them to visit!

***

Earlier today I had the great pleasure of my lovely friend Margaret visit for lunch and for a great afternoon - which almost went into early evening - of chatting and reminiscing.

Along with a bottle of wine, she came 'armed' with a photo of me and my church choir some twenty-five years ago shortly after I'd gone to Paignton Parish Church, which had been given to her by a former choir member and former organ pupil of mine. I've just been looking at it and thinking how so many of them have passed to their glory now.

There were some characters!

***

I have greatly enjoyed having friends Ivonne and Malcolm around to supper this evening. I tend to ignore the famous Mrs. Isabella Beeton's advice not to leave too long between courses (she pinched most of her writing from Eliza Acton anyhow!) and enjoy leisurely food. The evening lasted for about four hours or so, with us talking, reminiscing, and laughing between courses, and enjoying a single malt on the armchairs and sofa afterwards.

Over the last few weeks I've been privileged to cook for some lovely people (and still have more to come!) - and haven't poisoned any of them (yet!).

***

Recently my friend Petra and I were discussing some favourite pupils we had over the years. I mentioned one of my favourites - Sarah - who I taught the piano from a youngster until she left for university. Petra suggested that I might try to find her on Facebook. So I did, and sent her a message (hoping it was the same Sarah and not somebody else!). She replied to say she was the correct one, but isn't often on Facebook, and I think from what she said she enjoyed hearing from me, and I was delighted to receive a friend request from her. She also says it's weird to be calling me 'Gareth' and not 'Mr. Perkins' nowadays. It's been lovely to be back in touch after a number of years.

***

I've enjoyed a very pleasant evening. After the choir rehearsal, our newest (and youngest) member Megan was chatting, and agreed to come for a drink in a local pub afterwards. She only joined the choir as I said I would play the organ for her wedding on the condition she joined us! (Due to ill health, my organ playing isn't very good nowadays, but seems to manage to fool a lot of people.) She seems to be enjoying singing, and has reduced the average age of the choir by quite a lot! When we sat down, I said "Meg was born at an early age. Fill me in on the rest of Meg's life since then" (which is the sort of thing I say to people to get them talking). And she did. It was a fascinating evening listening to her life story, whilst she grinned from ear to ear telling it. I am so fortunate to have lovely friends.

***

I very much enjoyed lunch with three lovely friends Fr. Sebastian, Andrew and Petra. Fr. S. and Andrew went to the same school (just down the road from me and now sadly demolished), and it was lovely to listen to them reminiscing. Afternoon passed into early evening whilst we talked and laughed, and I was left reminded of how precious the gift of friendship is.

***

My mother and stepfather returned home late last night from a three week holiday, which they thoroughly enjoyed. My lovely mother 'phoned earlier and - in essence - the 'phone conversation went thus:
Her: "The internet's broken."
Me: "What do you mean?"
Her: "It's not working."
Me: "Ok. Are you not able to get emails or look at web pages?"
Her: "No, neither of our tablets is working, nor is the computer."

Me: "Have you checked that the router is switched on?"
Her: "It was working yesterday when we could get emails."
Me: "Ok, but you were in Turkey then. Have you definitely checked that the router is switched on?"
Her: "Yes. It's all wired up, but nothing's working."
Me: "Are you definitely sure the router is switched on?"
Her: "Yes!"
Me: "Are you 100% sure?"
Her: "Yes!" So I went up to try to sort it. And guess what...!

***

Random Thoughts, Wise and Otherwise

I've just enjoyed finishing watching Cardiff Singer of the World. Some really lovely performances.

But I've never enjoyed the idea of music being used in competition. When I was in my late teens (and could perform reasonably decently - unlike nowadays, alas) my late teacher kept trying to encourage me to enter local competitions as he thought I'd win. I really don't like the idea of somebody winning, and making others feel somehow not up to the mark, and upset. Music exists to give people pleasure, surely?

I've felt the same about grade exams ever since one of my young pupils - years ago - received a merit in an exam, having received distinction in his previous exams. His mum started to cry. I thought she was delighted - as he and I were - until she started shouting "How dare they only give him a merit?" several times. I saw his smile disappear and tears form in his eyes, and I had a hard lesson trying to convince him that he'd done well and wasn't a disappointment to his mum.

Why not just make music for the pleasure of each other, not compete, not have to pass the requirements of a syllabus, but just be able to make people smile because they're enjoying the performance?

***

At our vicar's request our organist and choirmaster played a certain voluntary (BWV 565) yesterday morning, which he'd not played for years and had hardly any time to brush up. One of the assistant organists turned pages, and two of the others went into the body of the church to listen. The assistant who turned pages praised the performance, as did the other two. The other two also sent flattering emails this afternoon. He enjoyed exploiting the kaleidoscopic new colours of the rebuilt organ (88 speaking stops), and the antiphonal effects from one end of the church to the other. Utterly tasteless, but great fun!

***

Yesterday we celebrated our church summer fayre. There was a good attendance, and a good time was had by all - to use 'clergy speak'! It will be interesting to see how much money was raised. I hope it's a lot. Our stall towards the organ fund raised £145 (or, rather, it will have done so by the time we've received the promised £3.50!).

One of the organist team - who ran the bouncy castle - was described as having such an inviting smile which would encourage all of the youngsters to have a go (he's a brilliant teacher, and I'm sure his students are very fortunate), and the organist and choirmaster on the organ stall was told he could sell sunshine to Arabs once he'd cajoled one lady into purchasing much more than she'd intended! He was ably assisted by another of the assistant organists and one of our friends, who did a superb job chatting with folk and selling stuff.

Another of the assistant organists was called by the vicar to help judge the dog show!

A lovely fun day and - after a little rain when setting up - the weather turned out to be kind to us all.

***

This morning at the church where I worship there was a service for the local school. It was lovely to see the youngsters there, and to hear them join in enthusiastically with the spoken and sung parts of the service. Our vicar was on fine form, and seemed to be enjoying himself. The piano was used for the hymns and for the Gloria, with another of our organist team singing to the youngsters before they sang themselves. Afterwards, the organ thundered forth with the Bach D minor Toccata - the 'vampire' piece - and absolutely shone. Some youngsters were asking the vicar where the sounds were coming from.

I thought to myself that just maybe the youngsters - who seemed to enjoy it, and who applauded and cheered the two of our organists team - were inspired enough that a few might become future members of the church, perhaps even choir members, priests, or even budding organists! Who knows?!

***

At the church where I worship there was a funeral earlier today. Very well attended. When the coffin was being carried out, there was loud and sustained applause from the congregation. The organist and choirmaster couldn't resist pulling out the new Cymbelstern stop on the west gallery (which sounds like bells ringing rapidly) to add to it. Great fun!

***

At church today we had a wedding. Apparently one little toddler started conducting - in perfect time! - to the first hymn. Wow - he could be a future musician!

At the end of the service whilst the bride and groom walked out there was lots of applause and cheering, so the organist decided to join in with the fun, pull out the Cymbelstern, and jazz up the traditional Mendelssohn, with syncopations and other utterly tasteless things to add to the fun! Apparently many in the congregation were bopping around to it.

***

I am greatly enjoying watching the televised version of the play 'An Inspector Calls' again, starring the brilliant Alastair Sim, and a fantastic cast. Should you not know it, it's a very clever play. The family's collective conscience appears in the form of a police inspector who arrives during supper one evening when they're all feeling smug, and reports the death of a young lady who had taken her life. He meticulously pulls each one of them apart, and shows them the bad that they had all done to this person to cause her to take her life. But we never know exactly whether it was the same young lady.

Towards the end they discover from a police officer that he's not a real inspector, and an imposter. All apart from the two young siblings, everybody else becomes smug again, until they receive a 'phone call saying that a police inspector is coming to visit them all concerning the death of a young lady. By which time, Alastair Sim's character has disappeared, just leaving a rocking chair he'd been sitting in inside a room from which he couldn't have escaped moving gently. The play ends. Brilliant stuff!

***

I enjoy teasing - and being teased.

Yesterday when going to church to see our organ builder who is completing an absolutely magnificent rebuild of our organ, I saw Mandy my next door neighbour. She said she'd not seen my beard looking as bushy before. I said I'd not seen hers looking as bushy before either and she laughed! I apologised a minute or so later after chatting, and she said she knew me well enough by now to know that I was teasing. She asked my friend Petra - who was driving - to do something useful, such as pushing me off Berry Head!

***

At church our vicar Fr. Paul came up to chat with me and the organ builder. The organ builder and I started talking in technical terms. Fr. Paul didn't understand what on earth we were talking about, and said something like "Right, I'm off", and I teased him by saying "That was the desired result!". I later emailed and apologised in case he thought it rude. But he also knows me well enough by now, I hope!

***

Many months ago we had a visiting preacher. After the service, I was chatting with the priest. Fr. Paul approached with one of our assistant organists - Mike - and I heard him say quietly to Mike "Let's tease Gareth". I thought to myself "Bring it on, mate"!

He said to me "Well done! You played far fewer wrong notes than the previous time you played". I replied "No, well done YOU. That sermon was the best one you've ever given by miles!". There was much merriment around the organ console, particularly from the visiting preacher (who had given the sermon) who called out "Touché"!

I am expecting my notice of excommunication any day now.

***

At the church where I worship we have two Sunday morning services. One at 9.30 which is designed to be family-friendly, and then the main one at 10.30. This morning we had a church fairly full of brownies, guides and scouts for the 9.30 service. The organist was on the piano, and one of the assistant organists on the electronic organ next to it (so they could see each other, rather than using the large pipe organ). Another had a tambourine. (Purists look away now!)

The vicar had asked the organist before the service to make the music especially exuberant, and to play them in to exciting music whilst they came in with their banners. Be careful for what you ask organists to do!

So the service started with an extemporised antiphonal fanfare between organ and piano, starting with the organ, whilst they processed in. The organist decided the key, and then the assistant was a right so-and-so and kept going into weird and wonderful keys for the organist to copy and lead on from the piano! Great fun!

At the end I'm told that one young lad leapt up and applauded with excitement. Perhaps a budding organist?

***

At this late hour, I've been sitting on the sofa watching an episode of As Time Goes

By - a most gentle and delightful comedy (why don't they make comedies like that nowadays?).

***

The dog has been snuggled up on the sofa next to me and snoozing. I heard the cat flap I had installed in the lounge door open. Madam had come in. She then decided to jump over the arm of the sofa to have a snuggle with me without realising that the dog was already there. She landed on the dog. The dog woke up with a start and objected quite vociferously. Madam shot back through the cat flap and has gone out into the garden, and is refusing to come back in. It's quite funny because - when they think I'm asleep - they'll both snuggle up to each other on my bed. Neither of them realise that when they're out in the garden, I stand at the top of the steps, and watch them being affectionate towards each other. She even went and stood by him when he had a poo at the bottom of the garden the other day!

***

At this early hour, a little ramble - which I hope might amuse you, dear reader.

Yesterday morning at the church where I'm privileged to worship, the 9.30 service was led by Fr. John Lee, who did a superb job. The service is meant to be family-orientated but, alas, there weren't any families there. The organist and choirmaster played the piano, whilst one of the assistant organists played the organ at the same time, and another one sat nearby feeling like a spare part; somehow we have attracted far too many organists (five!) - which has led the O&C to be teased about having a new hobby of collecting organists and denying other churches in the area of having them! It was great that the two of them would look at each other before reharmonising whilst they played, grin, and know what they were both going to do.

The O&C asked one of the assistants to play the organ for the 10.30 service, whilst he decorated and bashed away extra notes on the pedals. Intuitively, each knew what the other was going to be doing, and it sounded brilliant. Another conducted the choir, and another sang tenor. The O&C sang bass in the anthem. His singing was marginally better than his playing of the final hymn (which he'd been persuaded by the assistant to do) and a simple bit of Bach (which the three assistants who were there said they enjoyed).

We all left with enormous grins! Music is a great gift to us all. I'm looking forward to the dawn chorus which will start shortly. If you've never taken up music, go and find yourself a good teacher - you will never regret it.

***

Oooooh! It's snowing! Only lightly, but it's settling. As I live below the usual 'snow line' in Paignton, it's unusual to see snow here, but my back garden resembles a 'Winter Wonderland' at the moment. And I'm thrilled! At fifty years old, I'm still a child at heart. But isn't that the best way to be?

***

At church this morning two of our organists started extemporising a toccata on "O come all ye faithful" as the final voluntary. A third member of the organist team was grabbed from the choir recession and invited to join in - three organists on one organ! A fourth member of our organist team then joined in at the piano. It was sheer madness, but thoroughly enjoyed by the congregation who applauded enthusiastically at the impromptu orchestra.

***

Yesterday I was privileged to have two lovely friends round to lunch. Gill and Geoff. We started off by Geoff making music on the piano, with us singing carols, and me doing a little bit of decorating on the top. It was great fun! Then they survived my cooking (thus far - as Gill has sent a message this morning to prove she's still alive). Whilst we were sitting in the lounge afterwards chatting away about various matters, I found myself thinking about what a wonderful gift friendship is, and something to be cherished.

***

Two days ago I returned to my beloved Torbay after eight wonderful days in Mauritius (thanks to a competition win). Much as I love Devon, part of my heart will ever remain in Mauritius. I've been pondering why that might be.

 i, The people. They were lovely, and couldn't do enough to help you. Society there seemed to work on the basis of mutual helpfulness.
 ii, The warm temperature. This really eased my spasticity and made walking easier, and lessened the constant pain.
 iii, The delicious food, and the desire of the waiters to provide more and more food and beverages. Everybody was so generous, and nothing was too much trouble.

But there was something else which made it so special, which I didn't pick up until the day before leaving. That day was spent on a boat going around the south side of the island. There was a lovely gentle breeze, warmth, and several splashes of sea spray when the skipper decided to go fast in order to give everybody a thrill. And then it dawned on me. The hotel was next to a beach, with a lovely sea view from the bedroom. The salty infinity pool which I enjoyed very much just seemed to melt into the sea. The boat skipper who came to say hello and ended up enjoying - I hope! - a good chat with me about different boats, boat-lover to boat-lover. The sea was a constant factor, along with clement weather which is not often found in the U.K. It reminded me of days when I used to sail my little boat Liza Jane before ill-health made me pass her on to a new custodian. It was just like the coastline here but, thanks to the weather, somewhat better.

It reminded me of the words of the late and great Professor Raymond Cattell (widely ranked amongst the top twenty psychologists of the twentieth century, although not without his critics - but who is without those? - who moved across the Pond to work with the eminent Edward Thorndike) who - like I - spent some time living in the West Midlands before moving to Torbay (the only differences are that he was born in the Midlands whilst I wasn't, he was a far better sailor than I, and he was far more intelligent than I - dammit!) explaining why he moved to Hawaii:

"So, I came to Hawaii... It is a wonderful place in which to spend one's declining years, where snow is unknown except on the tips of 12,000 feet mountains, and where the aloha spirit of mutual helpfulness prevails. And for me and mine it continues, for in its steady trade wind in the palm fronds, I breathe the oceanic breath of Devonshire." Replace 'Hawaii' with 'Mauritius' and that fits the bill perfectly.

***

War is never the answer, is it? Sitting somewhere comfortable, talking, making yourself learn to understand the other person's point of view, being kind, and agreeing to meet somewhere in the middle is.

***

This evening I have returned from a short holiday in Houston, Texas, thanks to a competition win. It was a huge amount of fun, seeing the space centre, the museum of funeral history (not anything like as macabre as it sounds), and the museum of natural science among others. Staying in the very fancy Hilton Americas (apparently the largest hotel in Houston - everything in Houston is large anyhow!) was great, and I even enjoyed the luxurious flight (Shhh - don't let on, as I usually suffer from flight phobia and I was once heard to pray loudly on take-off much to the dismay of members of the choir I was accompanying who were seated nearby!). The food was terrific - and huge - and I've probably put on at least half a stone.

But the very biggest treat of all was one incredibly excited little dog when his daddy came through the door a week after leaving him to be looked after by family and neighbours.

***

Probably to the horror of my more cultured friends reading this (which no doubt includes everybody!), I have enjoyed enormous pleasure from watching "Batman

Returns" on the television this evening.

I remember that when it came out when I was a late teenager, I took my then girlfriend to the cinema to watch it. The gorgeous Michelle Pfeiffer (who played Catwoman) shone even more brightly than the other brilliant actors. When she strutted her stuff in her black latex catsuit, jumped down in front of Batman, posed and said "Miaow!" an audible sigh of pleasure - and no doubt desire - was heard from the men in the cinema!

It was that day that I learnt that not only did my girlfriend have strong arms and a hard elbow, but she also had a very accurate aim - which she directed at my ribs!

***

The last couple of weeks or so have been "interesting". Three Thursdays ago I noticed a little jaundice under my eyes. By the Saturday my whole body had turned yellow. So, two weeks ago today I visited A&E. I was seen very quickly. I spent the day having various tests, and seeing no fewer than four doctors. I was told that I needed to see a specialist. The appointment came through very quickly, and I saw the specialist on the Tuesday.

He suspected it was caused by one of the antibiotics - flucloxacillin - which I'd been given to try to help my leg to heal after my fall. I had more tests and more bloods taken and, as I had no fluid in my abdomen, I was able to go home.

The following evening the 'phone went, and he said my blood results were "shit" (his word) and that I needed to be admitted first thing the following morning. He informed me that were I to leave it for a few days, I would either be seriously unwell, or dead.

So I was admitted to hospital first thing Thursday morning for treatment. My bilirubin levels had gone from 300 mmol on the previous Sunday to nearly 600 mmol the following Tuesday. The top of the healthy range is 12 mmol. All of my other blood readings were just as they were the previous time. So I had a week in hospital, being given stuff on a drip, and being wheeled off for more tests.

Gradually the bilirubin levels started dropping, but far more slowly than they'd expected. He spoke with his colleagues, all of whom concluded it was flucloxacillin which had caused the problem.

In my last few days in hospital, my white cell count continued to rise, as did my body's inflammation response, suggesting I had caught a virus. They scanned urine and did an x-ray of my chest, but couldn't find the source of the problem. So, despite that doctor telling me I would have to remain in hospital for a while, one of his colleagues said that he felt that going home would be safer than staying in hospital with all of the bugs going around, as I now have much lower immunity. He had caught a virus too! I need to return each week for more blood testing. My bilirubin levels were still above 500 mmol, but hopefully will climb down.

I'm available to do Hallowe'en parties by the way, and I almost glow in the dark. So I remain glowing yellow. Guess what unusual colour the clock face was in my room... Yup, yellow! I entertained all of the staff by pointing out how thoughtful it was of them to provide another face which matched mine!

***

I'm watching the television, and my friend and neighbour Katarzyna Boadle has been on "The Bidding Room" selling a toy monkey (an absolutely terrifying thing which screams, and bangs cymbals, and would scare the life out of most children!) which belonged to my next door neighbour Alena (whom Facebook won't let me tag due to some glitch). Kasia did a superb job of selling it to the dealers, and got the top price of the range at which it was valued. From her excellent performance, I think she could probably negotiate selling ice and snow to Eskimos and make a good profit!

***

I've just been reminiscing with a friend about a dear and late friend of mine, John Hopwood, who was a superb music teacher, with whom I spent many hundreds (perhaps thousands!) of hours enjoying coffee, and sharing meals. We were like father and son. John would sometimes 'phone me in the mornings a little before 11 o'clock to tell me that his dog Scharf had escaped from the garden because the postman had left the gates open, and would ask me if I would visit to try to find her. I was always referred to as "Scharf's favourite person". He said each time he'd put the kettle on for a coffee for when I'd retrieved her. I'd park my car at the rear of his home, and walk through his garden and call her.

Scharf was always close to the front garden gate when I arrived and called her. It never dawned on silly me that the garden gate was closed!

My friend who I've been speaking to has said "Don't you realise that he let her out to get you to visit for a coffee?". And she's right! I hadn't realised that dear old Hoppy did. It's a lovely thought which has filled me with delight, rather like my days of sailing when I'd notice a sudden bit of a wave which was quite probably caused by a wind many hundreds of miles away, the results of which were appreciated much later.

***

Yesterday my lovely aunt Carol undertook a 90 minute journey to my neck of the woods. With her driving (which is almost as bad as mine - and that's saying something!), I can only wonder at the carnage which lay behind her! She met up with my cousin Marie, and Marie (thankfully - rather than my aunt !) drove to pick me up to take us to see my mother Sylvia and my stepfather Michael for a lovely afternoon, where chatting flowed freely. I teased my aunt about her driving without mercy (she loves it really!) And then my mother turned the tables, and brought out some old photos, including me as a podgy little child (I'm still podgy, and still a child at heart).

Mother got revenge for Carol by telling tales about my younger days. One of which was about the day when I was about three or four years old, and my mother, grandmother and I went to Plymouth to do some Christmas shopping. I was apparently playing peek-a-boo with mother, and then disappeared. She and my grandmother searched around the store, and then went to Woolworths to see if I'd gone there, and had the manager ask people on the tannoy if they'd seen a little lad in a teddy bear suit.

What they hadn't realised was that this little lad had gone out of the store, noticed that traffic was being obstructed by a van parked on the side of the road, and that motorists were sounding their horns at each other as they tried to negotiate it. So, this little lad decided if the adults couldn't sort it out, he had to, and stood in the middle of the road conducting traffic in his teddy bear suit. "Cometh the hour, cometh the teddy bear" as the saying probably doesn't go! Control freak - me? In the end I was "rescued" and taken to the local police station. Mother learnt what had happened, 'phoned the police station, and was told to hurry up to pick me up as I was eating up all of their supplies. Apparently I complained when mother came to pick me up, as I wanted another cup of tea. The policeman who spoke with mother told her to put me on a ball and chain the next time we came to Plymouth!

Whilst we were chatting, I kept quiet for a few minutes, and my aunt commented on it (by teasing that I was being unusually quiet!). I was actually musing on the fact that I was so privileged to be sitting in the same room chatting with four of my five favourite people, and how fortunate I was. The older I get, the more I learn that the simplest of pleasures in life are the most precious. Treasure those who love you, Facebook friends, and reciprocate in kind.

***

This morning an organ pupil of two of our team of organists played some carols as an opening voluntary. She's the wife of the curate at another church in the area, and is learning quickly. Two of the team sat with her and decorated her playing, and registered for her.

For the 9.30 service which is family orientated, we had both organ and piano playing together, and another of our team bashing the tambourine in the jazzy Gloria.

At the 10.30 service which is more conventional, the electronic organ - which is nicknamed "The Thing" by the team - was used, as we're still eagerly awaiting the completion of the rebuilding of the pipe organ. One organist played, with another decorating from time to time. They swapped places for the choir anthem so that one organist could serve as the only bass in the choir. Afterwards, following the success of last week's "all-in" the original organist played some variations on the final hymn "Guide me O thou great Redeemer", one of which was somewhere between a rhumba and a tango, and got called a mango by another of the team, who joined in on the piano. We started off again with two playing the organ for the variations (amazing the telepathy that they anticipate what each other is going to do and go with it!), and another of our team was grabbed from the choir recessional again, so once more we had three organists on the organ, and another on the piano. Then the one on the piano grabbed the tambourine, and added it at opportune moments to the final variation. Sheer madness! But I looked at the congregation who all remained seated and listening (I think tey were stunned!), and there was lots of applause again at the end.

So, five organists had a go today. Our other member of the team is recovering from surgery, and I wondered what on earth would have happened if he'd been around, and what instrument he'd have played (two organists on the piano, I guess!). A few years ago the church couldn't recruit an organist, which left an aching void. Now they have a team of five (plus a student who wants to become involved). I suspect the vicar thinks that the void has been filled, but that the ache remains!

***

I've just been writing something in pencil, and have been reminded that my friend Petra frequently tells me that my writing is always faint when I use a pencil. I have tried to convince her that is because I have developed pianist's hands over the years to play delicately. Who am I trying to kid?! When I play the piano, it's like Les Dawson having a bad day at work!

***

Various Grrrrs!

Flippin' Amazon! I pay for Amazon Prime. I ordered something yesterday evening which was meant to arrive today. I now see that it's due to arrive tomorrow instead. This is the umpteenth time this has happened to me. It's not a life or death situation, but is irritating. If you pay for a service, you should expect to receive it. Should something go wrong - and we're all human after all - an email explaining the delay and apologising would be welcome.

***

Whilst sorting through some stuff, I've come across a carrier bag. On it proclaims "The Co-operative bag: Make the most of it, it's not going to be around for ever. From date of manufacture, the plastic will start to degrade in approx, (sic) 18 months (sic) time. The whole process will take about 3 years. See bottom of bag for date of manufacture." As the bag is as good as new, I did. The date of manufacture was January 2010. Pah!

***

That moment when it's just before 5 a.m. and you're cuddled up to your dog under the duvet. You wake up, and then a few moments later hear all of the many clocks in your house chime five within a few seconds of each other. You're happy, and think all is right with the world as you've got them set up well. You snuggle with the dog again and start to drift back to sleep. Two minutes later, and one ruddy cuckoo chimes late, and you suffer the compulsion of having to return downstairs to make sure the ruddy thing will be on time should you be awake at six!

***

I am an absent-minded nitwit!

Noticing that my beard was becoming long and scruffy, I decided it needed cutting before attending church this evening. So I plugged in my electronic clipper and started hacking away. When I looked in the mirror halfway through I thought "What the heck?!?". I'd forgotten to put the plastic bit on the end which determines the length of the cut. It's not the first time I've done that. Unfortunately, 'designer stubble' doesn't cover any three of my chins!

So I'm now going to be attending church and looking as if I've forgotten to shave this morning! Tsk, Perkins!

***

I have been musing on the benefits - and otherwise! - of Facebook. I think it generally to be a gift. I have come across kind people who have subsequently become friends in the real world, and with whom I enjoy meeting up. I have come across former teachers of mine who have become friends. A former headmaster from my infant days said he would like to meet up. I have come across people who performed in concerts with me who have become Facebook friends. I have come across former pupils and become friends (I've really liked recently getting in touch with one of my favourites). (And - dare I say it! - I quite like reading posts from former girlfriends who have sent me friend requests; I think I may have been a randy chap in the past!)

There have been a few moments which I haven't enjoyed, such as a former friend who I'd looked after when she came on holiday here (which she repeated several times, with me almost always paying the bills for food and drinks - at quite a price, as she could eat and drink for gold in the Olympics!) - I'd gone around various guesthouses to find the guesthouse to meet her fussy demands, but she later told me that I was lucky that she'd only deleted me and hadn't blocked me due to a friend making a negative comment about the NHS and me not replying, a former friend who turned abusive when I replied to his chatting me up to tell him that I was heterosexual. And then an organist who had sent me a friend request (where I found that he would post about how much vodka he drank) who was subsequently rude to me, and to my aunt Carol and others who came to my defence.

And now to return to the kitchen after this little muse to prepare two of the puddings, the soup, and the melba toast for my friends Malcolm and Ivonne who are visiting tomorrow evening for supper. Friends should be treasured. I just hope the cat doesn't hit or bite them...!

***

This morning I went to hospital to see a consultant who I've seen various times over the last year or two thanks to illness. I was hoping that he might have been able to help out with my recent health difficulties. The receptionist was very apologetic and said that the strike by junior doctors had impacted on his clinic and that his appointments today have been cancelled. She said I was the second person this morning who hadn't received a letter saying that their appointment had been cancelled and had suffered a wasted journey. I am apparently on the 'pending' list.

After leaving the hospital I saw a small group of junior doctors standing outside with placards. I found it very difficult to have any sympathy for them. Surely there are more professional ways for medical professionals to ask for more money - if really necessary - than impacting upon the care of their patients.

***

I am flipping fed up with Amazon at times. I am sorry that it and other online companies are closing down our local businesses, and I realise that I'm part of the problem in using Amazon, but needs must with my mobility nowadays. There are some things which can only now be bought online unless one wants to treck quite a distance to find the desired product. A vicious circle. Again this evening I learn that my order to which I was looking forward to arriving by 8 p.m. - using Amazon Prime - is now delayed and is expected to arrive between 7th and 11th of April. I had another of these messages a while ago, and the order never arrived (I managed eventually to claim a refund).

Grrr, grrr and thrice grrr! Add a quadruple grrr for good measure.

***

Oh flippin' heck - this ruddy cold weather! Not helped by the fact that I returned from a competition win for a holiday in Mauritius - where it is presently their summer - earlier this week. I need to go for a shower shortly, so that the pong doesn't offend fellow worshippers at church too much tomorrow (thank goodness we use incense!). I also had the electricity and gas bill to pay earlier today for the last month and a bit, which was horrific - made even more so by the realisation that I wasn't at home for nearly two weeks of it. Gulp!

Roll on summer 2023! In the meanwhile - brrrrr! I have entered another competition for a holiday in Mauritius...

***

I know I'm going to sound like a scratched record repeating itself as I've posted something like this before, but I so hate noisy fireworks due to the effect they have on my lovely dog Milo. This year for some reason they've affected him even more than before. As soon as it starts to get dark he now starts whimpering and barking as he did when the fireworks were going off, even though they aren't now. I think the poor little lad is just anticipating them when it becomes dark and is scared. He is inconsolable and I don't know what to do to comfort him, because even sharing a biscuit with daddy (he tends not to eat after dark after the fireworks despite daddy munching on it and trying to show him that I'm enjoying it) and snuggles don't work. He is very stressed, effing noisy fireworks. Ban them now!

***

A couple of years or so ago I bought a load of adhesive hooks to fit in my kitchen so I could hang various lightweight items on them. Each of the ruddy things has gradually been failing one by one, and items have been dropping off. This evening I heard bang, crash, wallop from the kitchen. So I went out from the lounge to see what had happened. Another had failed, and a small colander had fallen from a hook on the side of a cupboard which had lost its stickiness, had evidently rolled along a worktop, and had fallen onto the floor. So I decided to replace the fallen hook with some better ones which I bought when the earlier ones started failing in order to replace them.

But answer me this, if you would, please, friends. Why is it when the glue is evidently not strong enough to hold a hook and something lightweight to the wall, it's well-nigh impossible to scrape the ruddy stuff off the surface from which the hook has fallen?

***

Flipping satnavs! Who would have thought that programming in "Newton Road, Newton Abbot" would have taken me to the edge of Dartmoor, and well away from the local town of Newton Abbot? There are some people who shouldn't be allowed out-of-doors, with or without a satnav!

***

Thank you to everybody who has taken time to wish me a happy 50th birthday (I feel old!). It's very kind of you and appreciated.

I usually try to respond to everybody personally each year, but I'm presently shaking off Covid-19 which has given me a bit of a thumping. I'm feeling better today - as if I've just got a common cold. But it's zapped me of energy, so I hope you understand that I've not felt up to leaving individual messages today, but just to leave a heart smiley to show you that I've seen your message and appreciate it. Hopefully I've not missed out anybody.

***

Today has been a very quiet day, much of it in front of the T.V. and watching "Florence Foster Jenkins" - one of my favourite films - which made me cry with both joy and sadness.

***

Well, It Amused Me!

This morning I was a passenger in a car. We stopped at traffic lights. All of a sudden we heard a loud bang, and the car behind us was bounced towards us. He'd been hit from behind. I watched in the mirror. The car which hit him reversed a few feet, and then bizarrely managed to lurch forward into the car once more and hit him again. The driver and his passenger got out and picked up some of their car's bumper from the road, before approaching the twit who'd managed to hit them twice.

Worrying that some people are allowed to drive, isn't it?

***

Please copy and paste this to your status for just one hour to show your loving support for those who are constantly being asked to copy and paste things to their statuses by people who copy and paste things to their statuses. I know many people won't copy and paste this, but my truly sarcastic friends will copy and paste it because it's in their nature to do such kind things because they truly have a heart. If you know someone, or have heard of someone who knows someone, you know what to do. If you don't know anyone, or even if you've heard of anyone who doesn't know anyone, then still copy this. It's important to spread the message even if no-one knows anything about anyone and it won't make any difference to anything whatsoever. If you don't copy and paste it, then this means you hate puppies. And if you hate puppies a unicorn dies. Possibly kittens as well. And occasionally baby goats.

***

It is said that little things please little minds. This is certainly true in my case! Having some family round for lunch this week and making crème brûlée as one of the puddings, I find that I'm unable to locate my mist water spray (used to stop the sugar burning too much), so I've been looking on Amazon for a replacement.

I have laughed inordinately at an answer to a question posted on Amazon: "Is this suitable for budgies" (no question mark) to which the answer was "The trigger will be too big for them to pull". It's just the sort of reply I'd have given!

***

I have just received two items of junk mail through my letterbox. One is from Cancer Research offering to write my Will for free, and the other is from the Co-op offering me a funeral plan. Is somebody trying to tell me something?

***

These insults are from an era before the English language got boiled down to 4-letter words. Insults then, had some class!

1. "I am enclosing two tickets to the first night of my new play; Bring a friend, if you have one." George Bernard Shaw to Winston Churchill. "Cannot possibly attend first night, I will attend the second...If there is one." - Winston Churchill, in response. .
2. A member of Parliament to Disraeli: "Sir, you will either die on the gallows, or of some unspeakable disease." -"That depends, Sir," said Disraeli, "whether I embrace your policies or your mistress."
3. "He had delusions of adequacy." - Walter Kerr .
4. "I have never killed a man, but I have read many obituaries with great

pleasure." - Clarence Darrow

5. "He has never been known to use a word that might send a reader to the dictionary." - William Faulkner (about Ernest Hemingway).
6. "Thank you for sending me a copy of your book; I'll waste no time reading it." - Moses Hadas
7. "I didn't attend the funeral, but I sent a nice letter saying I approved of it." - Mark Twain
8. "He has no enemies, but is intensely disliked by his friends.." - Oscar Wilde
9. "I feel so miserable without you; it's almost like having you here." - Stephen Bishop
10. "He is a self-made man and worships his creator." - John Bright
11. "I've just learned about his illness. Let's hope it's nothing trivial." - Irvin S. Cobb
12. "He is not only dull himself; he is the cause of dullness in others." - Samuel Johnson
13. "He is simply a shiver looking for a spine to run up." - Paul Keating
14. "In order to avoid being called a flirt, she always yielded easily." - Charles, Count Talleyrand
15. "He loves nature in spite of what it did to him." - Forrest Tucker
16. "Why do you sit there looking like an envelope without any address on it?" - Mark Twain
17. "His mother should have thrown him away and kept the stork." - Mae West
18. "Some cause happiness wherever they go; others, whenever they go." - Oscar Wilde
19. "He uses statistics as a drunken man uses lamp-posts... For support rather than illumination." - Andrew Lang (1844-1912)
20. "He has Van Gogh's ear for music." - Billy Wilder
21. "I've had a perfectly wonderful evening. But this wasn't it." - Groucho Marx.
22. "He has all the virtues I dislike and none of the vices I admire." • Winston Churchill

***

That moment when you've returned home after an evening with two very dear friends after a choir rehearsal (one of whom gave me a big hug at the end of the evening; I only wish he had been a hot, twenty-year-old blonde female with a nice figure and not a male of my age!), you fall asleep on the sofa having only had two pints in the pub with them and got evicted at a late hour from the pub after much laughter between the three of us (honestly it was only two pints!), and you wake up to find a dog and a cat cuddled up either side of you, and you decide to post about it on Facebook. You then find yourself wishing that they were both hot young blonde wenches too.

***

I have a number of clocks around my home. Some of which I've restored. Some of which are partially restored. But I still find myself checking the time on my wristwatch or pocket watch even after they've all chimed. There's no cure for stupidity, is there?

***

I had a 'phone call on my landline earlier. I loathe the telephone, but recognised a number which has been trying to scam me for a while, and decided to have a bit of fun...
Her (after a pause, and with a heavy Indian accent): "Er, hello?"
Me: "Er, hello?"
Her: "Er, hello?"
Me: "Er, hello?"
Her: "Er, hello?"
Me: "Er, hello?"
Her: "Er, hello. I'm 'phoning from xyz 'phone service to offer you a new cheaper plan for your landline, and to erase all of your debts to us..." (at this point, she waffled on with some complete and utter rubbish)
Me: "But I'm a mountaineer, and am halfway up a mountain, and can't receive any calls from my landline at the moment"
Her: "(Gurgling noises whilst her brain tries to compute what I have just said whilst she's speaking to me on a landline). What do you mean?"
 Me: "Well, I've tried stretching the landline up the mountain, but it won't stretch this far, so nobody at all can contact me by telephone. Not even you. I'm totally out of contact range. So there's no point in me having a landline because I can't use it, is there?"
Her: "(More gurgling noises whilst her brain imploded). Ok". She hung up. In retrospect, I should have played the gormless wonder for a lot longer and enjoyed it!

***

I'm presently sorting out a load of laundry, with the television on in the background. I got to the job of sorting socks, and was grumbling at myself for - yet again - not doing it during the daylight. As I did so, a lady on the TV made a comment about another contestant wearing odd socks. He said he never bothers to match them up, and just wears the first two he reaches out of the drawer, and it makes life a little bit more interesting for him. I'm wondering if it's a bit eccentric to take up that idea, even for me!

***

My friend Petra - who talks twenty to the dozen, and who has an extensive collection of donkeys' hind legs - has gone down with the same cold bug that I have. She is croaking and coughing when she tries to speak, as am I. I suggested she should rest her voice. She asked how long she should rest it, as she has a choir rehearsal to lead on Sunday morning. My reply of "I suggest resting it completely for the next five years or so, and then see how it goes" didn't go down very well.

***

Just when I was contemplating that my life probably couldn't get any more bizarre, I woke up this morning to receive an email from my lovely mother offering me a brand new toilet seat - as one does, I guess. (Just for the avoidance of any doubt, I feel I should mention that all four toilet seats in my house are immaculate, and very comfortable too!).

***

Petra posted this:

This is just too good not to share on Gareth's page. Earlier today he saw a tiny money spider crawling on him and thought that he had brushed it away, very gently of course so as not to cause it harm. He felt tired this evening and needed a rest. A few minutes ago he said that he felt something on his face. "I've got a spider building a web on me!" he said as he brushed bits of web from his beard!

Only Gareth!

***

I took a cardiologist friend of mine out to lunch today and we were both recalling anecdotes from our careers. His were perhaps the funnier!

He told the tale of one of his patients dying in hospital, and him having to sign the patient off as dead. So he went to the mortuary to inspect him, and found him stored high on the top shelf, so he wheeled the body out of the storage place, and the corpse fell out with a loud crunch right onto its head, doing some considerable damage. My friend concluded that if the corpse hadn't been dead before, it most certainly was deceased after that! He said it was one hell of a struggle to get a stiff corpse back onto the top shelf on his own. In the afternoon the local coroner came around to give a presentation to a group of medics, and chose this corpse. As he went around the body, he noticed the top of its head had been stoved in. Then he told them that this appeared to have happened after death, and asked if anybody knew how it had occurred. My friend made the excuse of having to take an important 'phone call, and hurriedly left the room. Nobody was ever any the wiser.

The second one was a patient who was wired up to a machine post-op. My friend noticed that her heart seemed to have stopped beating. So his training kicked in, and he thumped her hard on the chest. Nothing happened. So he did it again. What happened next came as much as a surprise to him as it did to his seemingly-late patient, who opened her eyes and demanded to know "What the **** do you think you are doing?". It turned out that one of the cleaners had been around with a vacuum cleaner, had unplugged part of the equipment to plug in her cleaner, and had forgotten to plug it in again.

And there was me thinking it was only me to whom these sorts of bizarre things happen! Thank Gawd I didn't train as a cardiologist...

***

I love people-watching! (Nope, I'm not a stalker!)

This evening whilst approaching a supermarket parking space, a fellow walked right across in front of the car, so engrossed in his telephone conversation that he didn't look to see if he was stepping into traffic, and didn't realise that he was. As he carried on walking - still totally engrossed in his 'phone conversation - his wheeled basked tipped over and emptied its contents in the car park. Undaunted, he righted his now nearly empty basket as best he could with one arm whilst continuing his 'phone conversation, and leaving items on the ground.

Having unlocked his car, he went back - still engrossed in his 'phone conversation - to pick up his shopping. His priority was an enormous pack of beer, which he struggled to pick up whilst still on the 'phone. Having struggled to open the back door of his car with one arm occupied with the 'phone, and the other struggling to hold the beer as well as opening the door, he struggled to get the beer onto the back seat of his car with one arm. He returned to the rest of his shopping, and picked up as much as he could manage with one arm, and began to carry it to his car. When his final trip was over, he went back to pick up some flowers he'd bought. I was amused to think that his priority was to rescue his beer, and what he'd left until last was flowers for his missus.

Looking at his flowers in one hand - and still engrossed in his 'phone conversation in the other - he realised that the flowers hadn't come through the ordeal very well.
So he walked back towards the supermarket with them in his one free arm, evidently hoping that the supermarket would swap them for some which hadn't got broken in the car park.

So, still engrossed in his 'phone conversation, he walked in front of another car, totally oblivious to that one too.

As he walked into the store with the flowers, he somehow activated the alarm. But he wasn't phased in the slightest. He probably didn't notice that either, as his 'phone was still stuck to his ear. I wondered how he'd manage to explain to the shop assistant why he wanted an exchange, whilst still continuing his all-consuming 'phone conversation.

I wish I'd videoed it, as it was such a wonderful performance of unintentional, unchoreographed farce. Sometimes Schadenfreude is such a deliciously guilty pleasure.

***

Looking at woodworm killer on Amazon for a small bookcase I inherited, it tells me that if I enter a code at the checkout, I can have the spray gift wrapped at a 50% reduction. It leaves me wondering who on earth would buy a bottle of woodworm killer as a present and want it gift wrapped, or am I missing something?

***

Sitting in the passenger seat in a car parked outside a shop this lunchtime whilst the driver went in to pick up an order, I was surprised to have the driver's door open, and a man climb in. I said "Hello" and he looked at me in surprise, started, and said "Oh ****! I've got in the wrong car again. Sorry!". He looked very sheepish as he climbed out apologising. He then walked to his own vehicle behind, which was a car-sized van, climbed in and drove off. Much to my amusement, it was a white van; the car that I was in was blue. I wondered if he manages to go through the correct front door when he arrives at home, or whether his neighbours are used to receiving an uninvited visitor...

***

Well today marks 12 months without drinking a drop of juice, fizzy drinks or any alcohol. Eight months without eating bread, pasta, cake or anything sweet. Sugar has been eliminated, as has caffeine and I follow a mostly plant based diet. The change in my body has been fantastic, I feel great, I have lost loads of weight and my way of thinking is very positive. No alcohol, eating extremely healthily and above all, a couple of hours of exercise daily!

(I don't know whose status this is, but I was so happy for them, I copied and pasted it.)

***

I've just been enjoying a chuckle about what one of our organist team at the church where I worship told me.

He's a semi-retired eminent cardiologist. He found himself one day inadvertently singing to himself "The day Thou gavest, Lord, is ended" whilst treating a patient. The patient glared at him and demanded to know why he was singing that! He thought quickly and tried to get himself out of the fix he'd inadvertently landed himself in by saying "Because you're my last patient of the day"! I'm so fortunate to have witty friends.

***

I've just had a good chuckle at a memory - and I hope you might too!

Years ago when I had my former and beloved little boat Liza Jane on the River Dart, I'd spent the night on her and had to get back to Paignton Parish Church that morning to play for a big funeral with our choir in attendance.

I set off in my dinghy to the pontoon at Stoke Gabriel (where I'd left my car), and found to my dismay that there were loads of dinghies off the end of the pontoon, with not much room for mine. I found - to my increasing dismay! - that they were all half full of water from the night's rain. I had to secure the painter (the rope from the front of a dinghy) to the end of the pontoon. So I decided there was nothing else I could do other than to climb into one of the dinghies in order to climb over the others in order to get to the end of the pontoon.

I only had one job to do - cross over several dinghies which were half filled with water. I failed! The first one sank with my added weight in it, and I suddenly became a swimmer with a bit of rope in his hand!

I managed to secure my dinghy, and get to the parish church - absolutely sodden and stinking of fish (and goodness knows what else - the River Dart wasn't too clean back then!).

Nobody batted an eyelid at a sodden organist who was giving off a terrible stench!

***

With the increase in fuel prices, I'm putting on extra layers of clothing in the evening. I presently have on three jumpers. It dawned on me a moment or two ago that I still haven't removed my tie. I suspect that I've been the only person in Paignton this evening wearing a bow tie and a hoodie together! Do you think I'm going to start a trend?

***

That embarrassing moment when you're doing your Friday evening housekeeping of emails you've received through the week to ensure you haven't missed any, and you find that you were evidently going on autopilot when you were replying to both your mother and the vicar at the same time, and you signed the one to your mother without putting a kiss at the end, but you put it on the email to the vicar by mistake.

I'm told he's booked another priest to celebrate Mass this Sunday morning...

***

My mother likes nauseatingly drippy greeting cards, alas, bless her! I got reprimanded for giving her a straightforward one a while back. So, as a tease, I've been calling her "Mumsy-wumsy" in emails. (Please don't call for the men in their white van and their straitjacket - they'll only find my front door bolted!).
She sent me an email where she'd typed "Goodnight, Godless" by mistake.
My friend Petra typed to me and meant to call me "Bigfoot" with my swollen foot, but her typing is terrible, and she called me "Bogfoot" instead! So I've been signing myself off on emails to my mother as "Godless Bogfoot".

I phoned my mother earlier and left a message on her answerphone. She emailed me to say she'd responded and left a message on my answerphone. The only problem is that there was no message on my answerphone. She'd evidently dialled the wrong number. So some unfortunate person somewhere in Paignton will have received a message saying "Hello Godless Bogfoot. It's Mumsy-wumsy here" and will have had their mind blown!

***

I've just been enjoying reminiscing about concerts I've been involved with in the past, and some daft people I have known, which you may enjoy, dear reader!

One of those concerts had me playing the organ to accompany the choir for the first two or three pieces (whilst our accompanist and deputy M.D.) took my place and conducted, before returning to the piano whilst I directed the rest of the concert.

We had a good audience, and I said some words of introduction, and went up to the organ to accompany. Imagine my horror to find that the first of the music scores I'd left on the organ stool had gone! I searched desperately for it, but it was nowhere to be seen. The deputy M.D. was poised and waiting for the first piece to start. I had to go down and apologise to the audience. I said I would have to pinch a copy from one of the choir, which I did. Imagine my surprise when returning to the organ console to find that that copy had my registration marks in!

I asked the daft fellow during the interval how he'd had my copy. He said that when he arrived, he'd realised he'd left his copy at home, but he'd noticed a small pile of music on the organ stool and that a copy of the piece he'd forgotten was on top of the pile, so the twit decided to take it. For once I was lost for words!

***

ACTUAL WRITINGS ON CHARTS IN HOSPITALS

The patient refused autopsy.

The patient has no previous history of suicides.

Patient has left white blood cells at another hospital.

Patient's medical history has been remarkably insignificant with only a 40 pound weight gain in the past three days.

She has no rigors or shaking chills, but her husband states she was very hot in bed last night.

Patient has chest pain if she lies on her left side for over a year. On the second day the knee was better and on the third day it disappeared.

The patient is tearful and crying constantly. She also appears to be depressed.

The patient has been depressed since she began seeing me in 1993.

Discharge status: Alive, but without my permission.

Healthy appearing decrepit 69-year old male, mentally alert, but forgetful.

Patient had waffles for breakfast and anorexia for lunch.

She is numb from her toes down.

While in ER, she was examined, x-rated and sent home.

The skin was moist and dry.

Occasional, constant infrequent headaches.

Patient was alert and unresponsive.

Rectal examination revealed a normal size thyroid.

She stated that she had been constipated for most of her life until she got a divorce.

I saw your patient today, who is still under our car for physical therapy.

Both breasts are equal and reactive to light and accommodation.

Examination of genitalia reveals that he is circus sized.

The lab test indicated abnormal lover function.

Skin: somewhat pale. but present.

The pelvic exam will be done later on the floor.

Large brown stool ambulating in the hall.

Patient has two teenage children, but no other abnormalities.

***

I know it's far from a laughing matter, but there are times when one needs a smile. I was listening to the television news a little while back about President Volodymyr Zelensky's visit to the U.K. and was in despair about the awful warfare. My gassy little Staffy was sitting next to me, with his rear end facing in my direction. He suddenly - and loudly - let off one of his worst ones yet. It made my eyes water, and made me leave the room in as much of a hurry as I could manage. And then I came up with a solution to the warfare. I shall seek arrangements to have him parachuted into Russia as an act of germ, chemical, and stink warfare, and only agree to take him back once all arms are put down. I think I have a very strong weapon with which to negotiate! What think you, friends?

***

A few months ago, I was looking for my previous mobile 'phone to use as an MP3 player. I hunted high and low. In the end I gave up, sorry to have lost it. It seemed to be a decent 'phone, hadn't had more than an hour of use, but had to be abandoned because it was a Windows 'phone and I - in my ignorance and disliking of 'phones - had bought it, not realising that there were no apps being written for it, as everybody had moved on to Android and Apple. Not being able to find it anywhere, I concluded that - unlike my usual behaviour of not throwing away anything which might have a future purpose in life - I must have decided to have binned it. So, I bit the bullet and decided to buy another 'phone for the purpose of being an MP3 player.

This afternoon I hunted around for three missing napkin rings to complete the set. When I got to the very last drawer to look through in my dining room and lounge (and there are a number of them!), I was delighted to discover the missing napkin rings. "Yay!" thought I! I wondered what was in the box next to them. I lifted it out and opened it. You don't need me to tell you what was in it, do you, dear reader.

***

More Randon Thoughts

As some friends will know, I had a fall a couple of years ago which caused damage to my leg, including cellulitis and all manner of problems. It hasn't ever fully recovered, not helped by being prescribed a large dose of flucloxacillin which caused me to be admitted to hospital, and subsequently caused oedema after organ failure.

Oedema has caused my legs to start ulcerate, which is flipping painful. I have a deep hole in one leg. I am having regular treatment for it, though, and I am being referred to a specialist clinic. But there's a nice side to this story! It's true that many clouds have silver linings. The nurse who treated me superbly this morning at my local doctors' surgery said that she remembered me from the hospital, where she used to work on the ward to where I was admitted.

She said she only ever remembers the most lovely of patients (sorry - that sounds big 'eaded!) and recalled me very well.

I remember during the time I stayed there my consultant telling me that I was the only patient on the ward who got up and dressed for breakfast (with deliberately nonmatching brightly coloured socks, and a bow tie which was deliberately never perfectly tied in order to show that it was genuine), and that I would tend to have almost a queue of nurses waiting outside my door to be "chatted up" (they tended to come and sit in my room and have a good natter; hearing some of the patients they had to put up with, I could appreciate they needed a break. And I enjoyed company too!). The lovely nurse and I chatted about all sorts today, from her mum's pets to my pets and various other things. She spent her time grinning from ear to ear, as did I. She was incredibly kind and thorough in her job.

I was reminded of the importance of being kind to others. Not only did the lovely young lass have good memories of looking after me during my time in hospital, but I recalled good memories too (I knew her face rang a bell). But, also, there might be times in the future when you'll be glad you were kind to somebody, as they might remember that time and be kind to you too.

***

I have just come into the lounge from the kitchen, where I have been preparing lunch for my lovely friend Margaret. In preparing one of the puddings, I had to open a new tin of black treacle. Would it open? Heck, no; not for several minutes at least. One of my dessert spoons eventually emerged triumphant from the battle as did I, but now looks as if it has suffered the unfortunate ministrations of Uri Geller (the spoon that is, not I)!

***

One of my former adopted strays I nicknamed "The Great Bashing Beast of Old Paignton Town" because he would thump anybody at any time. The only time he would be affectionate would be when I used the loo before bed and he'd come for a fuss and allow me to pick him up and snuggle him. At other times - no way!

***

Petra wrote:
Gareth just came into the sitting room with a doggy dental stick in his hand. Instead of handing it to Milo though he held it out for me! Not quite sure what this says about me or poor Milo!

***

Reading the news this evening, I wonder how long Liz Truss is going to survive as prime minister (albeit solely in office, but no longer in control). What's the betting she'll be gone by the end of the week, if not tomorrow? If she has any decency in her, she'll step aside, and soon. If the Tory party has any decency left in it, they will call for a General Election, retire utterly beaten from it to lick their wounds, to reflect on a number of mistakes over the last few years, and to regroup to be a balancing force as an opposition party.
I write as one who regards himself as a 'compassionate Conservative' and as a former party member (who always voted Conservative, apart from the one time I voted Green as a protest vote), but who saw the light a few years ago once the scales started to fall from my eyes, and I realised that the direction of the party had drifted too far from my ideals of common decency and improving the lives of all people. Or, perhaps, I had drifted too far from theirs.

***

Was Gareth in luck with this friend request?

I have received the following email. I think I'm luck here, don't you? Woohoo! She seems a bit malnourished, though. "Hi Hello my new friend How's your day? How's your day Nice to meet you:) Nice to meet you! I would like to meet you How do you look to learn more about each other? I would like to get to know you. In real life, I would never be the first to speak to a man, by nature I am shy, I think that the Internet makes it possible to communicate without hesitation. For me, it's easiest to talk on the Internet and you can not be ashamed of each other, but if our correspondence goes further, I would be glad to see you and get to know you personally, we could continue to write and get to know each other! I'm a pretty girl with blue eyes, I'm 5.6 feet tall, and a slender blonde. I am blonde with blue eyes, slim build, 5.6 lbs. I would like to tell about myself, My hobbies are reading books, going to the gym. I like volleyball, swimming, camping, skiing. I think you don't mind if I share facts about me. I love spending time at home, watching movies. I love comedies, especially with Jim Carrey, one of m yfavorite actors. I like to walk outside in the park, ride a bike or ski in winter. Have a nice day! Have a joyful day filled with fun:)"

***

Petra's Post:

Gareth's friends will, no doubt, have enjoyed reading about the exploits of Milo and Scaredycat. This morning I don't think that Scaredy was flavour of the month as I heard Gareth calling her a feral git!

The Reply:

Madam jumped on my bed last night, and was purring loudly whilst I was fussing her. All of a sudden she lashed out at my wrist with both paws, and has given me several puncture wounds. So, indeed, she's a feral git! (She jumped on my bed again later, poked me in the face to wake me and to try to get me to fuss her, but got ignored!)

***

Yesterday I went into town to have a set of bifocal spectacles fitted (which are going to take some time to get used to; I can understand my aunt Carol saying she couldn't use hers as they kept making her fall over), which have certainly improved some of my vision. Indeed, when I looked in the mirror after arriving home to see what they looked like, I could see so many more grey hairs than before. The joys of progressing towards one's dotage, eh?!

***

I'm having a friend visit for lunch today (the unfortunate fellow doesn't know I'm a cannibal!) and I've turned out onto a plate one of the puddings - a creme caramel. Despite having made it umpteen times to the same recipe over the years, this ruddy one has broken on its way out to the serving plate and looks awful (I've tried a bit, and it tastes good, though!). I'm wondering whether I should just serve him an apple. But, at this rate, there'll probably be a worm in it...

***

My lovely little dog Milo is often incredibly bright. He's also often incredibly stupid! I'm preparing some side dishes for a friend who is coming for lunch tomorrow (I hope he arrives in good time so that I can marinade him; he's not exactly in the first flush of youth, shall we say?, and could be a bit tough). Milo was being a pain and scrounging for food from me. So I threw one of his favourite biscuits down the garden to get him out of the way. Milo ran down to it, decided instead to have a pee right next to it on the path where it had landed, found that his pee had gone onto his biscuit, and decided he didn't want it any longer. Thank goodness for hens who love eating scraps! I only hope that they will have forgotten what they have just witnessed when they get the biscuit later!

***

I've this afternoon enjoyed laughing with my mother Sylvia Badcock and my stepfather Michael Badcock about my loathing of P.E. at school. At primary school, I had a tendency to hide my P.E. kit inside a bush on my walk to school, and pick it up on my walk home. At secondary school, I would make excuses about feeling ill to my mother to get her to write notes to get me excused from lessons. Once I'd collected enough of them not to arouse suspicion (the P.E. teachers were always daft enough to return them to me), I'd cut the dates off the top, and would keep them to be used in rotation. I lost count of how many verrucae, stomach bugs and sprained ankles the P.E. teachers thought I had suffered.

Before I did that, I organised a piano lesson at secondary school each week right in the middle of the P.E. lesson so that once I'd got changed into my P.E. kit, I'd have to change back. Then, once the piano lesson was over, I'd walk slowly back to the P.E. lesson at the other end of the school, get changed slowly, and then (if I'd timed it sufficiently carefully) find that the lesson was at an end, and would then get changed back.

***

This evening I have enjoyed an eclectic supper of reduced items from the supermarket. Some sweet chilli noodles, some potatoes, some cabbage, some carrot batons, and some cream. The noodles found themselves accompanied by a bubble-and-squeak of the vegetables and cream. I don't think Gordon Ramsay will be likely to offer me a job anytime soon (entirely his loss!), but it was quite delicious, even if utterly unusual. Perhaps Heston Blumenthal might be interested.

***

In other news, I have hanging in my downstairs loo from a gas pipe one of those hangers you use in a shower cubicle to store shampoo, soap, &c. It was relegated to the downstairs loo when it started to go rusty. It has on it two bottles of mould remover, a bag of wet wipes, an old toothbrush, and this evening now has one of my collection of cuckoo clocks and a barometer hanging off two prongs on the bottom of it. I think it looks quite fetching, and something of which Albion Nord would be very proud. And there are people who have the audacity to accuse me of eccentricity! Pah!

***

This afternoon I attended a funeral at my former church (where I was organist and choirmaster for a total of twenty years). RIP Anthea - a great character who, although gone from this world, was a force for good, and who isn't going to be forgotten in a hurry by anybody who had the privilege of getting to know her. (Nobody dared get on the wrong side of Anthea!) It was rather difficult to hear somebody else playing "my" organ (although I've moved on since then, and I am very happy at my new spiritual home where very exciting things are happening with the rebuilding of the organ there). I'd redesigned her in 1998 and she was rebuilt to my specification, and over the years I helped to maintain her, and quietly paid quite a lot of money out of my own pocket for our organ builder to do maintenance and improvement work on her. Not criticising whoever was manfully playing his way through the music today, but I had a great desire just to go to the organ bench of my former sweetheart and to tell him to move aside, so that she and I could have given everything a flourish - particularly Jerusalem at the end - which Anthea would have loved! Instead, I sang the hymns loudly, and inflicted my singing on those around me! I was humbled to have so many people come up to me afterwards to say hello, and who all reminisced about the standard of music we had in my time there. With my health not being very good nowadays, my ego - such as it was - is very fragile. But it's been boosted again today. A number of old friends want to meet for coffee or a pint (I'd rather the latter!) RIP, Anthea - and thank you for being the lovely person you were.

***

My lovely dog Milo is turning grey and showing signs of his age (aren't we all). Each night he goes down in the dark to the bottom of the garden to do what a dog has to do. There are several sets of steps to negotiate, all with uneven steps, and I've been concerned that he may have a fall in the dark one night. So I've bought some solar lights for him. I've fixed them all of the way down the garden steps. It was lovely a few minutes ago to watch him, and to see how the lights switched on perfectly as he approached, and illuminated the way for him all the way down and then back up again. From the energetic wagging of his tail, it was obvious that he quite enjoyed climbing up and down the steps in the light for the first time. He won't understand, of course, what daddy has done, but this evening a certain dog in Paignton has really enjoyed his night time trip down to the bottom of the garden, and being able to see where he was going.

***

I have seen various posts on Facebook today about the train drivers' strike. Lots of people seem to be getting very cross about the fact that shareholders are making high profits, and are saying things like "It's time for us working classes to stick together and stop these fat cats getting so much money. It's all the governments fault. Let's show the government we won't be bullied. I'm with the train drivers" - except they usually articulate their sentiment less eloquently. I can sympathise with the sentiment to a degree But, when you consider the situation of the train drivers receiving an average salary of £60,000 (and a considerable increase over what they were being paid back in 2020), I have to wonder whether these people have their heads screwed on against the thread, if their heads are screwed on at all. Surely if they are concerned about the shareholders making too much profit, they should be campaigning for cheaper railway tickets. This would especially benefit those of us who could only dream of earning anything like £60,000 each year (over £70,000 if you drive for Virgin), thereby cutting the shareholders' profits and making railway transport cheaper for all of us, rather than supporting those who seem to think they need over £60,000 p.a. on which to live.

***

There are times when I think "It could only happen to me"! I frequently think I'm surrounded by lunacy, but it's slowly dawning on me that there is one common factor around all of the lunacy, and that that factor is me! Take, for example, what has just happened. I have a wooden box at the end of the drive which has a sign on it for selling eggs. My ageing rescued ex-battery hens aren't laying much nowadays, but surplus eggs (which are delicious) go there for friends and neighbours to buy and enjoy.Imagine my surprise this evening to find that, rather than putting post through my letterbox, the postman has decided to put it inside there instead! I guess he is probably feeling the heat, but isn't it his job to put post through the letterbox and not inside a box clearly marked for selling eggs, and which doesn't often get checked?

***

I understand that Larry may shortly be installed as an interim prime minister, and that Larry is going to appoint my Scaredycat as his deputy. Methinks they would do a better job...!

***

Here are some of Petra's posts

(There is quite a good reason for adding them to the end of Gareth's book and it is this: I have used a writing programme that does not make it easy to delete blank pages and so I decided to add some of my Facebook posts to fill up the remaining omes.)

***

My previous staffy dog loved baths. Milo doesn't! However the lad was a bit pongy so I tried to get him into the bath this afternoon. Not a chance! He was very frightened of the whole idea. So I thought that he might tolerate a warm shower. I tempted him into the cubicle with little treats of cheese and after three or four I managed to close the door. It's a huge double shower with a seat so there was plenty of room for me and dog. Then I turned the water on and he loved it! He started to relax and really enjoyed the feel of the warm water and doggy shampoo. Problem solved. He is now sitting on a large towel and looking a very happy and clean boy.

***

One that most certainly needs a mention is my latest book.)

"The Adventures of Three Rude Rodents, Ruffers, Stink and Topper."

I just had to base Stink, full name Peregrine Fetherington-Brown, and known to his pals as Stink upon Gareth! Stink is a fairly posh rat, well-spoken and with a distinctive style of dress. He wears a waistcoat and a gold pocket watch as well as a cravat at all times.

Remind you of anyone?

Thought so!

***

I enjoy reading poems and sharing favourites. This one seems sadly appropriate at the present time.

A Small Child Looks At His World After The Bomb Fell

I'm sure it was a dove that I saw. OK, so it wasn't white. It was grey and black, but it soared through the air with such joy that it must have been a dove.

Its voice was not as sweet as I'd expected. OK, so it growled through the air with its gentle beak held high, But I'm sure it was a dove.

I'm sure that it was snowing that day. OK, so the snowflakes were hot and burnt my face And stung when I took breath, But it must have been snow.

The storm was much more rough than I'd expected. OK, so it shrouded the ground with a dirty cloud of soot But I'm sure that it was snow.

I'm sure it was poppies that grew there. OK, so they were small and weak But they danced on the earth with such fun That they must have been poppies.

They were not as white as I expected. OK, so they were blackened and torn but they looked at the world with their message of peace So I know that they were poppies.

(Anon)

Not Anon really, of course, but one of my own poems. I might publish a selection of them in a book soon, complete with drawings.

***

This will, no doubt, upset some of my friends but I hope that they will read it with an open mind anyway.

I attend Quaker meetings when I can which is far from as often as I would like. I help with a church choir and give lifts to a friend who plays the organ at times at a CofE place so I am quite tied to doing this. I was sitting there today between directing a sung psalm and an anthem looking around at the marble, the stained glass, the pictures and other trappings and the embroidery and robes and wondering why all of that wealth is spent on the building and trappings when a simple hall would have sufficed for worship. There are poor people today and it has always been so. Why was it seen essential to spend many thousands of pounds on building churches when the poor could have benefitted instead? Do the worshippers gain from seeing all of the finery and furnishings? Surely they are there to worship their God and not the peacockery (Is this is not a word it should be!) of the surroundings? There are so many more things about which I don't agree but they may keep for later in this thread or another day

***

Petra has just had one of the best laughs in years! A twit on a music forum that she used to belong to posted ages ago that his piano was too loud. Petra and another friend, who shall be nameless, GP!!!, suggested to the idiot that he should stuff old cushions inside it. Today another silly member, who didn't take good advice offered about buying a piano, asked how to make her new instrument quieter. The said former twit advised her to do as he had done and to stuff pillows and an old duvet in it!

***

Imagine, for just a moment, a country in which the people had a voice; every vote counted; and politicians were running to be true public servants because they cared about the health of the nation not their own personal wealth and power.

***

Many years ago I developed a large abscess on a front tooth and despite the best efforts of the dentist it ended up needing a crown. Fifty years later it worked loose and fell off just a few days before a holiday and was cemented back but It was suggested that the root would need to be extracted now and a bridge fitted. That seemed the best option and it was almost finished but I had a small temporary denture to use before the bridge is fixed. This evening I removed that and placed it on a side table as it is not too comfortable. Moments later my beast of a dog was crunching something on the floor. I thought that he'd been given his dental stick. (He has one every evening.)
Later I found a piece of something pink on the floor. I realised what it was that he'd been crunching! My denture! So now I will have to go about looking like a halloween pumpkin until February 1st when the permanent bridge is due to be fitted. I have washed all of the bits that Milo left and will try to superglue them together again but think that I will need to resort to wearing a mask for the next few days.

Grrrrrrrrrrr, Milo! You're not flavor of the week.

***

I was wondering what my greatest achievement of this year had been earlier. I decided that it was finding out how to mend the washing machine that the local repair man said was dead and gone. The repair man said that the computers in this model were always going wrong and are too costly to replace. A search on Google found a code to reset it. This was several weeks ago and it is still running perfectly. It is rather like setting the key code for a car.

***

Mauritius

(Another of my competition wins!)

We travelled up to Gatwick Airport in style! Gareth had requested special assistance and because the train was so full they moved us to first class where we had free food and drinks. A really nice experience.
We had a taxi to our guest house in Horley. A lovely couple running it and we were made very welcome by Zarina, the wife. We had a comfortable enough room with all that we needed for an overnight stay and the husband, Mohamed, was our taxi driver the following day. He should have been doing standup comedy! He was so entertaining.
We had lots of help at the airport with flight assistance and we boarded an hour before take off. The plane was full to bursting. We were able to get our large case for the hold booked in very early so we had the day free to sit in drinking coffees whilst waiting for the boarding to begin. The flight was uncomfortable but we survived.
When we arrived in Mauritius, again we had lots of help and our taxi driver was there waiting for us with my name on a board. He was very pleasant too and suggested some places that we might visit. It was a good hour's drive from the airport to our hotel on the North side so we saw a fair bit of the island. The roads are good here but there are a lot of derelict partly finished buildings around. The North side seemed a little better and more prosperous.
I was surprised at how green the countryside is. I was expecting it to be dry and parched but it is far from that with lots of tropical trees and plants everywhere. We passed some roadside sellers with piles of bright red fruits on sale but I haven't found out what they are yet. (I found out later that these were lychees.)
Our hotel is beautiful. We had a guided tour when we arrived. The staff are lovely and can't do enough for everyone. We have set meals in our package but they have made lovely vegetarian meals for me. Their salad dressings are really good. The breakfast is a buffet one with so much choice and very good coffee.
It is a safe area to go walking and I have been to the town three times on my own. There is a very nice beach area a few minutes from our hotel where they have lots of sand and shelter and snack bars with all sorts of fresh fruit and local dishes. We have an infinity pool on the hotel rooftop. Gareth went this morning and loved it. Our shower is really posh with a tap, a basic shower head and then a waterfall one high up with plenty of hot water and some nice toiletries to use. This morning Lil, our cleaner, made an elephant out of towels and then used my owl pendant for his

headpiece. It was brilliant and made us both laugh for several minutes. We saw her later and congratulated her for doing such a nice job. Our room looks lovely. I was sad to dismantle the elephant but he had to go before my shower.

We booked an all-day taxi trip on one day. It was very reasonably priced for several hours of his time. It was a lovely way to get a feel of the island without having to drive oneself. The sugar museum was not to Gareth's liking at all apart from seeing the huge machines but I really enjoyed seeing and reading about the conditions of the slaves here and how hard they had to work. It was not until the the Dutch took possession of the island that there were really any settlers here and they had a massive rat and locust problem, sorted out by the introduction of crows and mongooses.

We went to the botanical gardens afterwards. A lovely place to relax and admire the trees. We met a stray cat too but had nothing to offer it unfortunately, as it looked very thin and hungry.

Our next visit was to the Château La Bourbonnais, an interesting one with one room, the dining room, furnished in English style while the rest was French. Some beautiful wall coverings there. I would love somewhere like that as my summer retreat, as would Milo.

Our last port of call was to a small Catholic church, not the oldest church that I had wanted to see, but it was very plain with white painted walls and oak pews and little else and I found it a most peaceful place, not unlike a Quaker meeting house. It was next to what must be the prettiest beach here where they have done a lot of filming for various movies, so we were told. Back for coffee and a small cake and then to rest before dinner.

The food here is good and our waiter is lovely and knows just what we want; sparkling water and a veg meal for me. There is a slight ant problem in the restaurant and at times they crawl onto the tables. One evening he came to brush away the crumbs on our table and I said "The Ant man Cometh" which amused us as he swept them away along with the crumbs.

On another evening we were invited to a cocktail hour before dinner. It turned out to be a Mauritian style buffet and a singer. It was a great evening with sparkling wine and cocktails around the pool area (I didn't have any cocktails.) and then a very good buffet with plenty of veggie things. The puds were particularly nice so we had to try them all, just to be polite.

I woke early the following morning and I spent some time looking for a trip for tomorrow, found one, tried to book it and failed because my mobile phone company thinks that I am a scammer out in India somewhere. I spent a good couple of hours online with chatbots and real people and still it doesn't work. I almost wrecked the sim card by having to remove it and then replace it several times but it doesn't seem to be sorted. Gareth ended up using his details to pay for the trip. It was supposed to be my treat.

We swam several times in the hotel pool and my swimming is getting a little better. It's years since I last went swimming. Tomorrow we are off on a boat trip to see dolphins. And so we did! A very early start with the alarm set for 5.15 and our taxi arrived at 6 o'clock to take us to the South to meet our boat. We met up with two other couples who were great company and made jokes about exchanging wives for camels and other such things. They were really nice people and are now Facebook friends.

The dolphins were there in huge numbers with lots just below the surface and some playful ones on the top doing leaps and showing off their moves. Then we went closer to the next island where there were lots of tropical fish to be seen as the water was crystal clear and quite shallow. Finally we had time to relax on the beach before enjoying a barbecue and a rapid and very wet trip back in the speedboat that certainly lived up to its name. We had time for another swim and showers before dinner. It is sad to be leaving such a beautiful island and people. Another five weeks here would be perfect! I must enter more competitions!

We had a better flight back to Gatwick as we managed to choose seats with more legroom and also caught an earlier train. It is very cold here and we are both wearing several layers of clothes.

***

It's almost time to deck the halls. The poor Hall family must be so fed up by now (Little things do amuse me)

***

It must be poppy time again. I found another of my poems that I had posted on Facebook.

My Child Unknown

What did you do in the war, Daddy? I died, my son, I died.
Were you a bold, brave soldier, Daddy? Oh no, my son, not I.

Will I be like you, Daddy, With my little wooden gun As I march along the pavement with my best pal, Harry Dunn?

I saw my best pal shot, son. He screamed aloud in pain And he cried out for his mother Who he'd never see again.

Did you shoot the enemies? My son asked as he smiled. My boy, I had to fire and kill another mother's child.

Mum said you died a hero on the battlefield that day. My son, I was no hero. Please don't think of me that way.

I died in terror, crying. My body ripped and torn And sadness that I'd never meet my baby, newly born.

***

Soon it will be time for our leaders to lay wreaths of red poppies at the cenotaph. How bloody hypocritical of them! Since 2015 a brutal Saudi air campaign has bombarded Yemen, killing tens of thousands, injuring hundreds of thousands and displacing millions creating the world's worst humanitarian crisis. British weapons are doing much of the killing. Every day Yemen is hit by British bombs dropped by British planes that are flown by British-trained pilots and maintained and prepared inside Saudi Arabia by thousands of British contractors. If our politicians really cared they would stop the sale of weapons to Saudi Arabia, stop British technicians helping the war effort there and help to end this inhumane situation. I shall wear my white poppy and continue to encourage others to do the same. Selling weapons is no way to bring about peace.

***

White poppies are worn in the run-up to Remembrance Day every year by thousands of people in the UK and beyond. They have been worn in this way for over eighty years. The white poppy stands for three things: They represent remembrance for all victims of war, a commitment to peace and a challenge to attempts to glamorise or celebrate war. White poppies commemorate all victims of all wars, including wars that are still being fought. This includes people of all nationalities. It includes both civilians and members of armed forces. Today over 90% of people killed in warfare are civilians. Those who choose to wear white poppies remember all those killed in war, all those wounded in body or mind, the millions who have been made sick or homeless by war and the families and communities torn apart. We also remember those killed or imprisoned for refusing to fight and for resisting war. (This is rather serious for a book that began in a lighthearted manner. Time to lighten the mood!)

**

As a peace-loving, anti-war, anti-drugs, anti-smoking Quaker why do I get a quadruple S on my boarding pass and patted down, searched and swabbed for explosives?

**

Iced coffee is not to everyone's taste but I love it. Earlier today I made myself a serving of it but drank only half. Later a friend, or perhaps exfriend now, reminded me about not having finished it and passed it to me. Which of us was to blame I do not know, (I suspect him!) but as I took it,the thing decided to hurl its contents over said friend, the dog biscuits, the food mixer and the floor! I hope that the dog does not become addicted to caffeine!

**

Rather than hijack a friend's post and further comments about the **Last Night of the Proms** I decided to add my comments here. Someone mentioned the irony of EU flags being waved whilst singing Land of Hope and Glory and I do see this. My thoughts are these: The words of Land of Hope and Glory were written before WW1 by Arthur Benson and were intended to celebrate the glory of war. Elgar's musical influences were not English but German, taking inspiration from the works of Handel and Brahms. His work is often said to be typically English but the choral works do show the mark of Brahms. I'm not sure that the opening lines are relevant now! "Thine equal laws, by Freedom gained have ruled thee well and long; By Freedom gained, by Truth maintained, Thine Empire shall be strong." I think that the empire was lost long ago and I am not proud of how it was won. The slave trade and conquest of poorer countries in order to build the British economy is questionable by anyone's standards and this was crippled by two world wars. So a strong empire now? No! If we remain a part of Europe we stand to continue to forge links with other EU member states by fair means, not foul. This having been said, the Last Night of the Proms is great fun and a chance to yell out some good tunes. Perhaps it is time to rewrite the texts of some though. There are some verses of God save the Queen that have been deemed inappropriate now and are not sung. I would like to see an alternative text sung, one penned by William Hickson:

"God bless our native land! May Heav'n's protecting hand Still guard our shore:
May peace her power extend, Foe be transformed to friend,
And Britain's rights depend On war no more."

I'd love to see these words replacing the anthem.

***

I'm getting annoyed with people moaning about the cost of things. £2.50 for a coffee, £1.75 for a tea, £2.25 for a cupcake....
If I hear any more complaints I'll stop inviting people round!

***

I am just wondering how someone with an allergy to nuts chooses to hang out with us! (I suspect that this post referred to our new friend, Mike Webb)

***

Just home from attending a concert with a friend. We bought two raffle tickets each and on checking them on the way out I found that I'd won something! Lucky me! I handed the man running it my ticket, number 17 and he looked at us and announced "Smellies!". I was taken aback and replied "We aren't, Fishface!"" at which he produced my prize; a box of smellies.

***

There are things that one never expects to hear at church fetes. We were selling teddy bears and a lady came to look at them all. She said that she had a theory that every room in her home should have an extra pair of eyes. I asked her if she had one in her toilet. A moment later little voice close to me piped up with "I'll be your toilet bear!" as he waved a teddy in her direction.

***

A friend was reading the draft of my latest book earlier and came across the plan for each chapter as well as the body of the book. I saw him typing madly and I see that he has, helpfully!!!!!!!, added an outline for a further chapter: Chapter Eleven They all fell down a well, and nothing more was ever heard of them, nor written about them!
Nice, eh?

***

This has been a great **Valentines Day!** Five bouquets of red roses, ten boxes of chocolates and three bottles of Moet! I might have been able to grab more but that security man at Morrisons was just a bit too fast and can he run!

***

Overheard in a charity shop in Bangor today: "
I met another Pagan today."
"You did?"
"Yes! I'm a Pagan. I thought O my God! "
And moments later:
"Jesus Christ, what's this?"

***

The prize bundle that I won arrived today and WOW! It's like a second Christmas! Lots of really expensive cosmetics. some lovely candles, room scents, perfumes Armani socks and pyjamas that have been gifted to a friend, and some baby and child items that have been given to one of our lovely neighbours as well as some wireless headphones and a car phone charger. Lucky me! I forgot to mention a fleecy blanket too! (I remember giving the poor man who phoned me to tell me that I had won a very hard time as I thought that it was a scam.)

***

Home after a great production of Mikado with Llio Evans and others in the cast and I haven't enjoyed a G and S more! It was modern, imaginative and great fun and a brilliatly funny "List" song. Any cast that sings "Bugger the flowers of Spring" gets my vote

***

Soon it will be time for certain groups to celebrate Diwali, the festival of light. This celebrates, amongst other things, light over darkness, good over evil, forgiveness and knowledge over ignorance.
Many will celebrate the gunpowder plot on November 5th. Might it be nicer to embrace the ideals behind the festival of Diwali rather than a failed attempt to blow up Parliament and the burning of Guy Fawkes ?

***

Today a friend and I delivered a couple of buns to some more friends as a treat. We had an email back to thank us. I have just read my first friend's reply:

"I hope you enjoy the buns. They were the last two left. They'd fallen on the floor, and a couple of children were kicking them around before we picked them up. We mentioned it to the checkout assistant, who kindly got out some tissue to wipe off the fluff and bits and pieces, and took 10p off the bill. Those assistants always seem to go the extra mile when sworn at."

***

How lovely to see a true professional enjoying his work! Gareth Perkins playing at a wedding of some good friends yesterday. That will add a certain something to the wedding album. This was taken at the wedding of two of our Anglesey friends, John and Ruth. It was one of our best days there

***

Mini Disaster at an otherwise rather good concert in Colwyn Bay this afternoon! I tried out my wooden basset recorder this morning and found it in need of cork under one key. I decided that it was too rattly to use and as it was just for one piece I took the trusty plastic Yamaha to use instead. I hadn't played it for a few weeks but trusted it to do the job. Part way through the piece the windway started to clog. There was no place to sort it out another way so I did a short suck-back. That always works! Not today! I should have cleaned it out first.

I started to choke and knew that I had swallowed a spider, hopefully long dead. My throat closed up and my eyes started to run as I tried to continue with the solo but I failed. I gasped to my accompanist that I'd swallowed a fly! He kept playing some rather pleasant variations as I tried to recover. Twice I tried to join in and failed both times. I grabbed my water and had a slurp and tried a third time, and managed some final notes. Then I thought it best to explain more fully to the amazed and amused audience what had happened.

***

A Final Post From Gareth

I have been asleep on the sofa for a fair chunk of the evening. My little dog woke me, and insisted on yet more food, despite the little podgy fella having had a generous portion earlier (he gets treats each day in addition to more food than a dog should have, and knows that he's loved). We did our usual routine of me sending him to "his place" which is halfway up the stairs, and then to "top". He nowadays pretends to object to running, but it's all part of his game (perhaps in challenging the leader of the pack; but he should realise that is the cat's position), and his tail wags loads. When he declines to ascend I pretend to be about to tickle him. He loves it, and then goes totally daft about running up and down the stairs. We continue the game until I can hear him panting. He has now had another tin of meat, and another scoop of biscuits. I thought he would be happy. But the little fella - hugely overfed and spoilt - has picked up his food bowl, walked into the lounge with it, and shaken it in my direction! I'm pretending I don't understand the message he's trying to convey.

***

I hope that Gareth, you have enjoyed reading these posts once more. Some amusing, some more serious, and some of Petra's for good measure. Keep writing and making your friends happy! Enjoy this mini album of my favourite photographs too!

This was a Christmas present a few years ago

Gareth and two friends performing The Cats Duet in Paignton.

No particular reason for this photograph other than because Petra loves it.

Gareth with Nelson, his parrot, all set for an event at Moelfre for Lifeboat Day.

Gareth! Always one for the birds!

Printed in Dunstable, United Kingdom